Why Turtles Have Shells

Story by Janie Spaht Gill, Ph.D.
Illustrations by Bob Reese

◆ **Dominie Press, Inc.**

There once was a turtle who had no shell in the days of long ago,

and so he had no warm, dry home, like the turtles that we know.

His name was Timothy Turtle,
and he took a walk one day,

to see if he could find a place
warm and dry to stay.

He came upon a bear cave.
He thought, "That cave will surely do."

So he asked the warm, dry bear,
"May I live with you?"

"My home is big," said the bear.
"For a turtle, a cave won't do.

You need to find a smaller home that's exactly right for you."

He came upon a bird nest.
He thought, "That nest will surely do."

So he asked the warm, dry bird,
"May I live with you?"

"My nest is high," said the bird.
"For a turtle, a nest won't do.

You need to find a home on the ground that's exactly right for you."

He came upon an ant hill.
He thought, "That hill will surely do."

And so he asked the little ant,
"May I live with you?"

"My home is tiny," said the ant.
"For a turtle, an ant hill won't do.

You need to find a larger home that's exactly right for you."

Walking along the shore,
Timothy saw an empty shell.

He thought, "That shell could keep me warm and dry. I think it would work well."

"This shell is not too big, nor too small.
This shell is not too high.

I think that it would work just fine.
I'll put it on and try."

Timothy found that turtle shell did keep him warm and dry.

Now all the turtles wear a shell, and that's the reason why.

Curriculum Extension Activities

Why Turtles Have Shells

- Have the children brainstorm a list of animals that have shells: turtles, tortoises, snails, crabs, clams, etc. Then have each child draw and color one of the animals listed.

- Help the children make a poster of animals that have shells.

- After the children have read *Why Turtles Have Shells*, make up word problems to go with the story: "There was one turtle. He met a bear and a bird and an ant. How many animals were there, altogether?"

- In the story, the other animals tell the turtle why their homes are not "exactly right" for him. Ask the children if they can think of reasons why a shell would not be "exactly right" for the other animals. For example, "If a bird had a shell, it would be too heavy to fly," or "If a bear had a shell, he wouldn't have a comfortable sleep during the winter."

About the Author

Dr. Janie Spaht Gill brings twenty-five years of teaching experience to her books for young children. During her career thus far, she has taught at every grade level, from kindergarten through college. Gill has a Ph.D. in reading education, with a minor in creative writing. She is currently residing in Lafayette, Louisiana with her husband, Richard. Her fresh, humorous topics are inspired by the things her students say in the classroom. Gill was voted the 1999-2000 Louisiana Elementary Teacher of the Year for her outstanding work in primary education.

Publisher: Raymond Yuen
Editorial Consultant: Adria F. Klein
Editor: Bob Rowland
Designer: Natalie Chupil
Illustrator: Bob Reese

Copyright © 2003 Dominie Press, Inc. All rights reserved. No part of this publication may be reproduced or transmitted in any form or by any means without permission in writing from the publisher. Reproduction of any part of this book, through photocopy, recording, or any electronic or mechanical retrieval system, without the written permission of the publisher, is an infringement of the copyright law.

Published by:

ⓔ Dominie Press, Inc.

1949 Kellogg Avenue
Carlsbad, California 92008 USA

www.dominie.com
(800) 232-4570

Softcover Edition ISBN 0-7685-2183-1
Library Bound Edition ISBN 0-7685-2491-1

Printed in Singapore by PH Productions Pte Ltd
1 2 3 4 5 6 PH 05 04 03

Dominie Level	Guided Reading	DeFord Assessment
20	L, M	9